THE
GEMINI
ORACLE

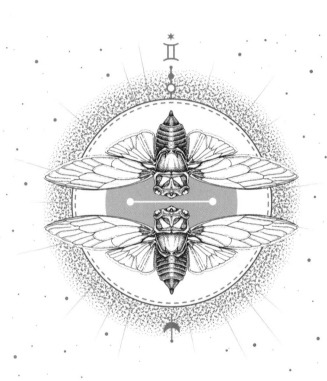

THE GEMINI ORACLE

INSTANT ANSWERS FROM YOUR COSMIC SELF

STELLA FONTAINE

greenfinch

Introduction

Welcome to your zodiac oracle,
carefully crafted especially for you Gemini,
and brimming with the wisdom of
the universe.

Is there a tricky-to-answer question niggling at you
and you need an answer?

Whenever you're unsure whether to say 'yes' or 'no',
whether to go back or to carry on, whether to trust
or to turn away, make some time for a personal
session with your very own oracle. Drawing on your
astrological profile, your zodiac oracle will guide
you in understanding, interpreting and answering
those burning questions that life throws your way.
Discovering your true path will become an
enlightening journey of self-actualization.

Humans have long cast their eyes heavenwards to seek answers from the universe. For millennia the sun, moon and stars have been our constant companions as they repeat their paths and patterns across the skies. We continue to turn to the cosmos for guidance, trusting in the deep and abiding wisdom of the universe as we strive for fulfilment, truth and understanding.

The most basic and familiar aspect of astrology draws on the twelve signs of the zodiac, each connected to a unique constellation as well as its own particular colours, numbers and characteristics. These twelve familiar signs are also known as the sun signs: Aries, Taurus, Gemini, Cancer, Leo, Virgo, Libra, Scorpio, Sagittarius, Capricorn, Aquarius and Pisces.

Aries   Taurus   Gemini   Cancer   Leo   Virgo

Libra   Scorpio   Sagittarius   Capricorn   Aquarius   Pisces

Each sign is associated with an element (fire, air, earth or water), and also carries a particular quality: cardinal (action-takers), fixed (steady and constant) and mutable (changeable and transformational). Beginning to understand these complex combinations, and to recognize the layered influences they bring to bear on your life, will unlock your own potential for personal insight, self-awareness and discovery.

In our data-flooded lives, now more than ever it can be difficult to know where to turn for guidance and advice. With your astrology oracle always by your side, navigating life's twists and turns will become a smoother, more mindful process. Harness the prescience of the stars and tune in to the resonance of your sun sign with this wisdom-packed guide that will lead you to greater self-knowledge and deeper confidence in the decisions you are making. Of course, not all questions are created equal; your unique character, your circumstances and the issues with which you find yourself confronted all add up to a conundrum unlike any other... but with your question in mind and your zodiac oracle in your hand, you're already halfway to the answer.

Gemini
MAY 21 TO JUNE 20

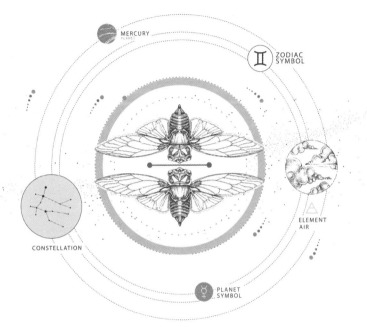

Element: Air
Quality: Mutable
Named for the constellation: Gemini (the twins)
Ruled by: Mercury
Opposite: Sagittarius
Characterized by: Curiosity, adaptability, sociablity
Colours: Yellow, green

How to Use This Book

You can engage with your oracle whenever you need to but, for best results, create an atmosphere of calm and quiet, somewhere you will not be disturbed, making a place for yourself and your question to take priority. Whether this is a particular physical area you turn to in times of contemplation, or whether you need to fence off a dedicated space within yourself during your busy day, that all depends on you and your circumstances. Whichever you choose, it is essential that you actively put other thoughts and distractions to one side in order to concentrate upon the question you wish to answer.

Find a comfortable position, cradle this book lightly in your hands, close your eyes, centre yourself. Focus on the question you wish to ask. Set your intention gently and mindfully towards your desire to answer this question, to the exclusion of all other thoughts and mind-chatter. Allow all else to float softly away, as you remain quiet and still, gently watching the shape and form of the question you wish to address. Gently deepen and slow your breathing.

Tune in to the ancient resonance of your star sign, the vibrations of your surroundings, the beat of your heart and the flow of life and the universe moving in and around you. You are one with the universe.

Now simply press the book between your palms as you clearly and distinctly ask your question (whether aloud or in your head), then open it at any page. Open your eyes. Your advice will be revealed.

Read it carefully. Take your time turning this wisdom over in your mind, allowing your thoughts to surround it, to absorb it, flow with it, then to linger and settle where they will.

Remember, your oracle will not provide anything as blunt and brutal as a completely literal answer. That is not its role. Rather, you will be gently guided towards the truth you seek through your own consciousness, experience and understanding. And as a result, you will grow, learn and flourish.

Let's begin.

Close your eyes.

Hold the question you want
answered clearly in your mind.

Open your oracle to any page to
reveal your cosmic insight.

Give yourself a break; even
though staying switched on and
firing on all cylinders can feel as vital
as breathing to you super-connected
Geminis, sometimes even you need
to dial it down for a bit.

With Mercury in charge, it
can be tough trying to take a step
back, but sometimes you need to let
all the buzz carry on around you. Take
a quick break and you'll be back in the
thick of it in no time at all.

When you know what it is
you really want, there is nothing
more powerful than that energized
adaptability Gemini is so famous for.

A little self-love never goes amiss, and Gemini you know you're worth it. In fact, you could probably hold back a bit, to be honest. You are all about taking care of yourself.

It might be that you are only
seeing the obvious with this one,
but honestly, isn't that what matters?
Everyone else wastes too much time
overthinking things like this;
let's just keep it moving, Gemini.

Ruled by Mercury, you love to
be on the move, and preferably
at a pace. But be careful you're not
zooming past this one too quickly –
take the time to look at this from
another angle, you might find that you
missed something first time round.

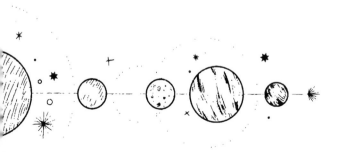

Change is coming Gemini. Stay light on your feet and nimble in your thinking, and you will adapt easily.

Balance is a tricky one
Gemini – sometimes it feels you
have finally achieved it, only for a
surprise to throw you off again. But
each and every time you have to make
your way back, it strengthens you
that little bit more.

Gemini is an air sign and you need to keep that oxygen flowing. Get out into the fresh air today – challenge yourself to an uphill walk or a long run by the sea – and the answer will reveal itself. This is a tricky one, but not for the reasons you think.

Much as you prefer thinking over feeling Gemini, let your gut instinct direct you on this one.

Quick, versatile and smart as
you are, sometimes you need to take
a pause and let the world catch up
with you. There is something you still
need to know, something you may
miss if you race on ahead.

Your Gemini obsession with information-gathering (and, let's face it, sharing) might not have served you well this time. It is important to investigate further. The details are not exactly as they seemed at first, fleeting glance.

Although it doesn't quite fit
with your lively and spontaneous
approach to life, this time you need
to acknowledge that there is likely
only one acceptable outcome.
Proceed with caution.

It's not about control as much
as the need to keep numerous plates
spinning, and of course there is no one
better at that than you. But you will
need to trust your stars for this one;
your path ahead is already illuminated.

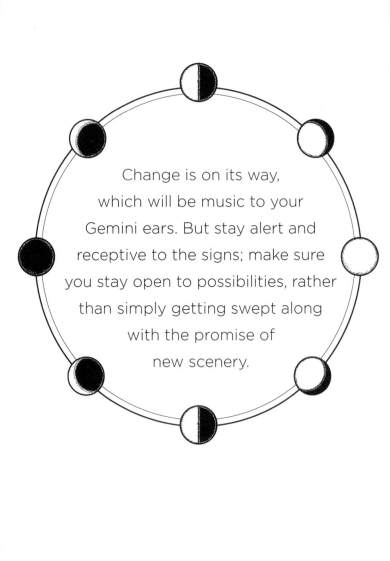

Change is on its way,
which will be music to your
Gemini ears. But stay alert and
receptive to the signs; make sure
you stay open to possibilities, rather
than simply getting swept along
with the promise of
new scenery.

Your Gemini love of a good
chat and a bit of digging will not
necessarily help you win this time.
Worry less about what other people
are thinking (and don't obsess over
the fact that they are clearly wrong);
you cannot control the feelings of
others. They will come to realize
the truth in time.

Difficult as it seems to play the long game, you must keep your powder dry and bide your time. A sequence of small wins will be the secret to success.

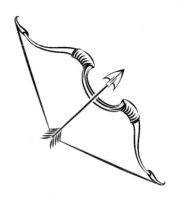

With Sagittarius as your
opposite sign, sometimes you
need to remember that a more
philosophical approach can yield
greater meaning and understanding.
Now is one of those times.

Neither patience nor persistence come easily to you, but they may be useful skills to harness. They could be the key to your success this time.

Your fullest potential is not
to be found in pursuit of popularity
and a constant social whirl, but in
nurturing and learning to understand
those who truly care about you.

Your warm and open manner puts others at ease Gemini. Don't take advantage of this, but rather understand that their sharing demonstrates trust.

If events and situations feel like
they are weighing you down, take
some time to let off steam and indulge
in relaxation and recreation. Enjoy your
friends. Get out into the fresh air.
Forget about more pressing
concerns, at least for a
little while.

Time to quiet your thinking brain
down and go with it; your first impulse
was the correct one, although initially
it may have seemed to make
little sense.

If this path is looking too difficult, think about whether what lies at the end is really worth it. You can always change your mind – and moving onto the next thing is one of your particular talents.

No one could ever accuse you of being boring, predictable or steady (the horror). But uncertain times call for a commitment to decisive action; now choose your path and get moving.

You already have all the knowledge
you need to make this decision.

It might be time to change
your thinking on this one, so it's
lucky you are so famously adaptable.
It is time to at least consider the
possibility that the first move you
made was, in fact, not the way to go.

Try to take a break and allow things to be as they are. The small things have a way of working themselves out.

Despite the thought you have
put into this, it might be one of
those situations in which actions speak
louder than words. So many of them
do seem to be.

Perplexing as it is, your Gemini
gift for seeing both sides sometimes
goes unappreciated; lean into your
intuition this time and keep your dual
nature to yourself. As well-meant as
they are, there is a chance your words
may be taken as unwelcome criticism.

You pride yourself on honesty and communication, but now and again a messy conflict does seem to make its way to your door. Resist the temptation to over-talk this one and package it neatly away in the 'wins' pile; just watch and wait.

Pat yourself on the back Gemini,
and have a roll around in that warm
feeling of pride in your achievements;
you are living life well. Let pleasure
rule this moment.

Understand that the feelings
you have now might not be the
same feelings you have tomorrow,
even though the issue remains the
same. The outcome may depend less
on your input or interference than you
first think. Give yourself some time and
space while you allow this situation
to resolve itself.

When you have worked out what you really want, no one is as talented as a Gemini at exploring all possible routes to make it happen. Just be sure you get hold of it quickly, before you change your mind again.

Usually you are the life and soul
of the party Gemini, and if anyone
knows what's going on when, where,
how, why and who's involved, it's you.
'Ear to the ground' doesn't even begin
to cover it. So, it can feel disorienting
when things seem not to be going
your way. But, as ever, there is a
greater plan at work here.
Be patient.

Breathe, stay in the moment,
let go of that you are seeking to hold
and this too shall pass.

If the support you need just isn't forthcoming, are you really in the right place? Put your own needs first.

Of course there are two sides
to everything, you know that better
than most Gemini. But you need to
focus on the positive and distance
yourself from any negative energy
others are putting out there; it will
block your path to success.

This situation demands you be
a little more forthright, possibly even
aggressive, in pursuit of the outcome
you need. Nothing should be allowed
to get in your way.

Certain changes can take some time to get used to, but retaining perspective is important. Consider whether what's been happening, and particularly your feelings about it, are really that significant in the greater scheme of things.

This is the perfect time to
celebrate how far you have come and
how much you have already managed
to achieve, rather than focusing on the
distance left to travel. Time for a party!
Are there any words sweeter to a
Gemini's ears?

Do not withhold your true feelings, even if you are concerned that expressing them may cause upset. Now is not the time to be stifling this kind of information – your ability to move forwards depends on speaking up.

Your flair for expression and creativity, and your quick wit, will prove invaluable in this endeavour. Just be careful not to let your tendency to change your mind or become distracted send you off course.

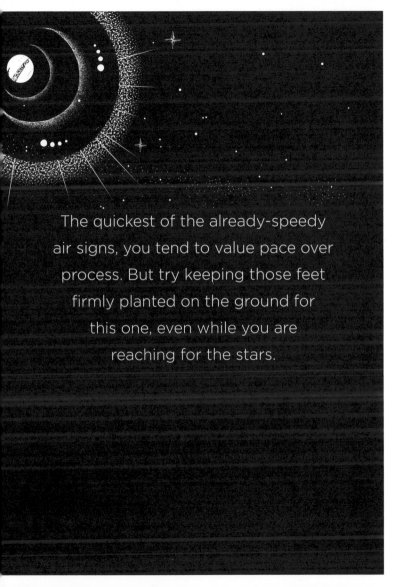

The quickest of the already-speedy
air signs, you tend to value pace over
process. But try keeping those feet
firmly planted on the ground for
this one, even while you are
reaching for the stars.

Now we all know that socializing is your oxygen and where there's a chance of a get-together you don't hang about. So, make it happen Gemini; it's time to pop the corks, turn up the music and really let your hair down.

Time for a blast
of fresh air Gemini –
you need to spend some time
in your element. Take a break from
the thinking and feel the wind beneath
your wings; maybe sailing, a walk out
on some blustery cliffs or a good
old-fashioned spot of kite flying. Time
to blow those cobwebs away and
let in some of the new.

Of course, anything is possible
for a lightning-quick, razor-sharp
Gemini. But you might need to look at
this one the other way round.
The direction of approach will
make all the difference.

Others can be complicated, but
no one loves socializing as much as
you do Gemini. Inside all those other
people are lots and lots of little bits of
information, and who better than
you to coax all those nuggets
to the surface?

Remember, not everyone likes having their secrets told far and wide as much as you love doing the telling. Although information-sharing is your most-beloved currency, others don't always feel the same way.

Try to allow someone else to help this time; they may well surprise you, and it might even make things easier.

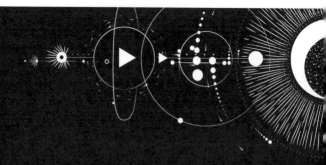

Time to try something
different. Listen, focus, notice,
feel, acknowledge, stay present.
It's harder than it sounds to resist
engaging with that mind-chatter
of yours, but it will do you good
to sink down beneath it all.

On this occasion, your dual
Gemini nature will be your ultimate
asset, helping you achieve a best-for-
everyone outcome. Let one part do
the thinking and the other do the
actioning. Rise above the detail and
it will all be done in no time.

You've never understood the grudge bearers, and they can't get a grip on how you can just allow their displeasure to slide off you like butter off a hot knife. Some things aren't meant to be. Onwards, no looking back.

Your reputation as the most brilliant company precedes you, and you never disappoint. But even you need some downtime occasionally, especially if you are to continue bringing your A-game. Keep it quiet today and you'll be ready to face your public again in no time at all.

Time to take a deep breath, grab hold of your courage and ask the right question. Your answer will be right there in front of you, as soon as you are brave enough to ask.

While all this feelings stuff isn't
quite your bag, you should follow your
gut instinct on this one. Your first
impression was correct.

Geminis are endlessly
adaptable, but you should know
that decisions to aim for big changes
are best not made on the spur of the
moment. Sleep on it.

You are what you do, not what you say. Sometimes you're moving so quickly you might not notice how many you are leaving behind in your wake. But don't side-step your impulse to maintain connections – it has never failed you yet.

Honest communication will not be mistaken for emotional manipulation. You have the ability to make people hear what you are saying, use it now to help them understand what you need and so improve your situation.

Deep and meaningful soul-baring chats, while an essential part of the way you function, are not to everybody's taste. Remember that everyone sees things differently. Suspend judgement, and, if you really must have your say, do consider all likely outcomes first.

Remember that a true friend is one who tells you what you need to hear, rather than simply what you want to hear. Loyalty and truth go together on this one. Although, granted, it is always a lot more fun to hear things that please you.

Resist your impulse to immediately spark up that social network to find out everything you can in your quest for the correct solution. Others' opinions will only complicate things. Pull out some patience and wait to see what the universe offers up in its own time.

Overthinking will be your enemy
on this one; resist it, lest it lead you in
a self-defeating circle.

Not all obstacles can be charmed, cajoled or chatted into submission; of course, your first impulse is to zip all over the place to fix this problem, but simply stepping around it rather than becoming tangled in a spiderwebby mess would be a more elegant, and much less sticky, solution.

There is a difference between
friendship and flattery. Not all signs
agree that smoothing the way is as
important as acknowledging truth.
Remember this.

Constantly resetting your
targets will mean you just end
up zigzagging about aimlessly.
Resist second-guessing yourself.
Your personal clarity and strength
of purpose will serve you well.

The situation might not be quite as it seems – adopt an inquisitive Gemini approach and take another look before you make your decision.

Your success will depend on doing
the very thing that looks right but
might feel counterintuitive. Let your
head rule over your heart.

It might be that you are finding
it difficult to get to grips with this
one. If so, press pause and disengage,
even for a short time. A little distance
will make all the difference and bring
some much-needed clarity.

You are an active listener,
curious about others and intuitive
enough to understand even the unsaid
things. Others feel heard when they
engage with you. But it is not always
essential to put your view across in
every situation; sometimes just
your presence is enough.

Duck away from the urge to pick
your path until you are sure you have
the right balance between thought
and emotion – head and heart are
both required in this situation.

Adversity always brings opportunities to a Gemini; you are adept at finding the positives and at hurtling into the right position before anyone else. See past the immediate issue to what likely lies ahead. You don't need to figure it all out right away.

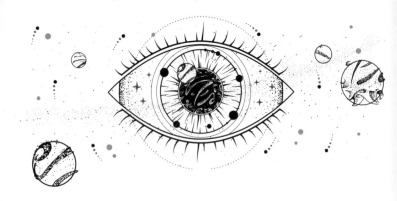

On this occasion, yes you can.

But that doesn't mean that you should.

Look carefully before you leap.

The story you tell is the one others hear; they cannot know what is in your heart unless you tell them.

Your future approach may
benefit from the lessons you are
learning now. That doesn't make them
fun, necessarily, but what comes next
will be entirely in your hands. Learn
from the past and move swiftly on.

The answer you seek lies directly
in front of you; do the thing you are
sure you won't regret later. That is the
greatest wisdom you can bring
to the current situation.

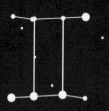

You will find a way Gemini, you
always do and there are plenty of
options. Perhaps take the easier
route this time if you can.

You're more of a sprinter than a marathon runner, and your ability to work quickly and move fast is unsurpassed. But bear in mind that people are different and most probably need an idea of where their reward might lie in order to knuckle down and get on with it.

It is never too late for an apology,
whether you are giving or receiving.

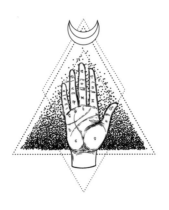

Too much talking without any
resulting action can frustrate you and
diminish your energy and momentum.
Don't allow those who are looking to
monopolize your time for their
own entertainment to break
your stride Gemini.

Don't be too suspicious of all the
hard work required this time, even
if it feels like it might not be worth it.
Something much easier is just around
the corner, so you can start enjoying
that very soon.

Find a way to carry on, even if
this wasn't part of your original plan.
Slowing your pace at this point will not
guarantee the greatest rewards.
Keep moving forwards.

Gentle and affectionate, energetic
and enthusiastic – Gemini is the most
dualistic of any zodiac sign. You are
twinned, after all. So, make the most of
your gift for seeing both sides at once
and take the most balanced approach.

The brightest of the air signs,
you know better than anyone the
importance of keeping things flowing.
Don't let anything (or anyone) get in
the way of your trajectory.

Don't forget that softer, more vulnerable part of yourself, which is the bit that really matters. Protect and nurture it.

There is a chance you are spending too much time trying to get to grips with this one, and that's just not your style. It won't affect the ultimate outcome, so focus your energies on something else.

Although zipping around the place treating everyone to a lovely dose of your fizzing, sparkly energy is clearly the most wonderful way to spend your time, this one demands a little attention. Don't fail through lack of focus.

Expand your talents out to meet the opportunities presenting themselves – you have many strings to your bow. You've never been shy, so don't step back from an opportunity that might have been tailor-made for you.

Slow things down for the time being – even though it might feel like something must be done immediately, set your impatience aside on this one. You will know when the time is right.

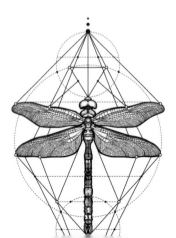

Your Gemini talents for
keen understanding, productive
communication and quick adaptability
will be in hot demand. Look ahead
and focus on the future.

Truth and wisdom are more likely to reveal themselves if you allow a little stillness in which they can surface. Silence and space are imperative if you are going to sort this one out.

Pull yourself together from
your centre, stop casting all around
yourself for whatever you can catch
and shake off that nervous energy.
Engage with structure, clarity and
intention. Stand tall, stay present.

Hold your tongue until you can
speak from a place of truth rather than
from a desire to receive a response.
Only then does what you want to
say actually need to be said.

You are ruled by Mercury,
the messenger, so have a deep
and abiding love of information and
communication. Your natural curiosity,
and energetic pace, make you a
particularly talented news-gleaner.
Use your skills.

Guard against your insecurities;
they will lead you into nervousness
and inconsistency, and become
an obstacle.

Making your point is crucial,
but spend a little time refining
your delivery. Remember to speak
from the heart, with compassion and
understanding for those you
are addressing.

Usually the life and soul of the party,
it can be a shock to those around you
when restlessness takes over and turns
to frustration. But it is important to
give both sides of your nature room
to breathe; neither is good or bad.
They just are.

You've a tendency to spark plenty of brilliant ideas, but you are perhaps not quite as adept at seeing them through to the finish. Being honest about this trait upfront will mean you can ask for the help you need and free yourself to concentrate your energies on the bit you're best at. Better for everyone.

Know yourself and keep a
mental checklist of the things you
need to do when routine closes in and
threatens your usual sunny outlook.
Keep moving, seek spontaneity,
talk it through. Above all, be
kind to yourself.

Like Castor and Pollux, the twins for whom Gemini is named, you are bold, curious, adventurous and resourceful. Use your star-given talents wisely.

The third astrological sign in
the zodiac, you are quick to take
the temperature of any group you join
and to adapt your energy to suit. This
chameleon-quality rarely fails you and
it keeps everyone else comfortable
too – three's never a crowd
when you're there.

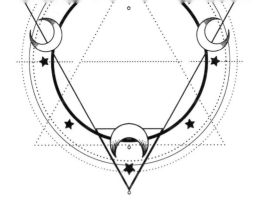

Highs, lows, whatever – as long as something's happening, you're happy. It's tedium that you must avoid.

Your inspiration and sparkly energy
are gifts made to be shared Gemini –
they will never be diminished by
allowing others to benefit as well.

Staying still is not in your nature
and with so many planets always
on the move through Gemini it's
no wonder you favour a dynamic
approach. Just be sure you let others
catch up with you once in a while.

A charming, fascinating, adventurous sign, you're up for grabbing hold of whatever life offers on that silver tray. Just be careful that all this focus on having fun today doesn't drain the bottle completely. Seize the moment, by all means, but remember there is a tomorrow on the way as well.

Focus on yourself and indulge in some self-care – the sooner the better.

The decision to give unsolicited
advice should not be taken lightly;
even when you are speaking from a
place of love and concern, your
observations may very well sound like
criticism or superiority to the recipient.
If you simply must speak out,
do it as gently as possible.

Avoid the things that stifle
you, whether they be repetition,
rules and routine, or that small-minded
approach that certain people seem to
bring time and time again. Let go of
that which does not serve you and
spend no time dwelling on the
unsolvable.

Collaboration is a huge Gemini strength, and with your gift for chat and incomparable charm there are few who can resist coming along for the ride... at least in the beginning. Put a bit more thought into the whole thing, rather than just the start.

Humility is important,
especially when others are
seeking your opinion. It's all too easy
to be swept up in the warm feeling of
others' admiration, but if they really
need your advice, you must take
your responsibilities seriously.

It is important to be honest
with yourself and others about your
ability to stay the course for this one
– don't promise anything you
won't be able to deliver.

Your usual habit is to move on quickly, and with so much out there still to experience, of course this makes perfect sense. But on this occasion perhaps you might be persuaded to linger a little longer; there are some aspects you haven't yet understood.

The most dual of signs Gemini,
it is essential that you balance the
mundane with the exciting, rather than
getting swept up in just the sparkly
stuff. When thrilling changes start
to take shape, enjoy them, just
don't forget the day-to-day
tasks that keep you going.

Keep one eye on the long-view
Gemini, remember you need to
build towards the future as
well as living today.

Teacher mode doesn't come easily to some, but there are many different ways to learn. Swap that high-energy, big-noise persona for a more introverted approach for a while and let your intuition guide you to where your lesson awaits.

There is a flipside to your life-and-soul-of-the-party spirit Gemini, as there is a duality to everything with you. Sometimes you turn inwards, you may feel anxious or even afraid, and there is nothing to do about this except wait for it to pass. Use this time wisely, seek silence and embrace the introspection. It won't last long.

Secrecy can breed suspicion, and anyway it's not your style. Although keeping it quiet might feel easier in the short term, embracing a commitment to openness and honesty is much more your brand.

Celebrate the success of those you love, with whole-hearted generosity. Their elevation will almost certainly serve to raise you up as well.

Good things are coming your way
Gemini. Hold tight.

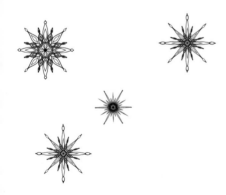

You should separate yourself
from negativity and bad energy,
whatever form it takes. Do not allow
others to fix you in place or, even
worse, drag you backwards. Now is
the time to speak up for yourself.

Support others, particularly those you love, through their own personal changes. It may take you some time to adjust to their new direction but allow them some space.

You may be butting up against opinions that seem super-fixed at the moment Gemini. Who better than you, with your gift for seeing both sides, to help others realize there is another way to look at this?

Much as you may secretly wish
to have all the answers Gemini, now
is the time to own up to all the things
you don't know, and perhaps even
ask for some help.

Focus on creativity Gemini (even
if you don't usually see yourself as the
creative type), with a big splash of
fun added for good measure.
Learning is much more likely to
stick when it's served up alongside
a bit of laughter.

You do not face your challenges alone Gemini, those you love are right there alongside you. They may be worrying about you, concerned about your stress levels, even if they do not say so. Now would be a good time to reassure them.

Maintaining distance between your work life and your personal life is a good idea Gemini – despite your strongly dual nature, you must appreciate the need for this separation. It will be helpful for everyone, as particular sources of tension should start to melt away.

There's no one as skilled as a Gemini at seeing both sides of an argument, but then you're often in two minds yourself... take a break from trying to figure it all out and lose yourself in a pleasant distraction (or two, you don't have to choose between them) for a while.

Looking forwards and backwards
at the same time is second nature to
you Gemini – the past holds many
lessons and the future holds
much possibility.

When seeking out new knowledge
and ideas, you don't always have to
look to new teachers Gemini. Those
you know well have been learning
and growing and gathering wisdom
alongside you. They might
even be willing to share.

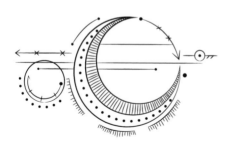

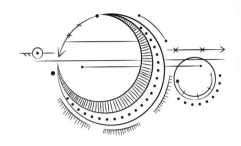

Fresh energy and ideas always
fill you with overwhelming enthusiasm
for the possibilities that lie ahead, it's a
rush like no other. But resist the urge
to neglect everything else in your
pursuit of the new; keep
your options open.

You are all light and joy and energy,
the life and soul of the party, Gemini.
Don't get too wrapped up in yourself
and the idea of your own popularity
though; it's important to maintain
a bit of substance underneath
all that flash and fun.

There are plenty of tricky people
out there and they may well test your
patience. But they are not you and
they have their own challenges; letting
them get under your skin would be the
height of foolishness. Onwards.

Without any respite, the journey
can seem long and arduous. But fresh
excitements are just around the corner
Gemini, and a new dawn is on its way...
you wouldn't want to miss this
one, would you?

Sometimes it seems that all
that feeling, and talking about feeling,
and acknowledgement of everyone's
feelings, can really get in the way. Set
your course towards logic and
decisiveness today and get moving.
Give your emotions the day off.

You are a deeply intuitive sign Gemini, but, like all your traits, intuition brings both rewards and difficulties. Right now, you may be finding it distracting, and so struggling to understand what you are feeling about particular issues. Focus on the practical and get through your day.

Bringing your intuition, intelligence
and innovative approach to this one
will mean you have it solved in no
time. Just don't move on too quickly,
even though it might seem to be
done; linger for a while
to be sure.

Life's one constant is that
everything changes. Breathe in hope
and light, and breathe out anything
that doesn't serve you.

Sunshine and smiles surround you right now Gemini, even if you are not aware of them yet; your positivity is starting to rub off on others. This is a remarkable achievement, all things considered, and you should not underestimate the impact it will have over the coming days and weeks. Things could have been very different... disaster averted.

Keeping that balance between
heart and head is vital for you Gemini,
otherwise it is all too easy to
get distracted.

Embracing a fresh point of
view will lead you into a place of new
open-mindedness that is full of
possibilities. Things will look very
different from that vantage
point Gemini.

Whether you feel your stars
are setting a welcome challenge or
testing you a little more harshly than
usual, you should rise to the
opportunity Gemini. You are more
than capable of taking this one
in your stride.

You are in demand; your imagination, intuition and creativity pretty much guarantee that others find joy in your company and like to be near you. You need only accept the best of them. Be selective.

All that goal-setting and hard work will pay off Gemini – rewards will be knocking on your door in no time. You've done what you need to do, now allow yourself the time and headspace to truly relish this next phase. You deserve it.

It is important to find your
focus Gemini; flitting between
options will burn you out and waste
everybody's time, as well as
exhausting their patience.

Work through as many tasks
as you can right now Gemini, ticking
off that to-do list will be satisfying as
well as freeing you up to enjoy the
excitement that is just around
the corner.

Feeling overwhelmed shouldn't
be a problem for you Gemini, in fact
there's something about being able
to showcase your unparalleled
multitasking ability at full throttle
that's quite thrilling. Time to
get on with it all.

Tuning out and taking time to
recharge is essential, and doubly so for
someone who lives life at your pace
Gemini. You will feel back to your
normal self in no time at all.

Extremely skilful at fitting in, no matter what the group or occasion, you are something of a chameleon Gemini. Your charm and charisma take you to the next level. Just be careful you don't treat this all as one big game. To you, perhaps it is, but others are involved and they deserve more consideration.

The bigger picture is the perspective you're most comfortable with Gemini, and it will give you the opportunity to avoid potential conflict and disagreement at the moment. Let the niggly details go and focus on pulling back for that wider view.

Friendships and relationships are sometimes as much about letting go as they are about holding on. Even if you don't agree with someone right now, it's perhaps not necessary to alert them to that fact. You're amazing at holding two views at once Gemini – flex that skill now.

Going along with things and doing them the way others seem to need them done is the right flow to follow for now Gemini; they may very well have their reasons.

Don't waste your energy on
the less important things right now
Gemini; save it so you have strength
for the things that really count
when they come around.

Sharing your time with your
friends is vitally important Gemini. Of
course, you are always trying to be in
two places at once, that's a given. But
when they need you, do everything
you can to show up for them.

Staying swift and responsive is as much to do with keeping your eyes open as it is to do with ensuring you are not unnecessarily encumbered. Stay nimble, keep your wits about you and don't miss what is going on.

Opportunity will come calling Gemini; you just have to make sure you don't miss the doorbell when it rings.

If dissatisfaction is gnawing at you, don't make the mistake of thinking that material things will fill that hole Gemini. The most they will do is obscure the problem for a short while, but sure enough it will be there again the next time you look. Look for a more meaningful, enduring solution.

Avoidance is simply storing
up problems for the future Gemini,
and time will only exacerbate the
issue. Best to sort things out now and
make a clean break or a fresh start...
possibly both.

Time to put yourself first Gemini;
leave any care for the opinions of
others to one side. Ultimately, they
need not touch you.

If there is a problem you have been ignoring, it looks like now is the time to turn and face it. Best get on top of it before it gets on top of you.

It's not like you to become trapped
by indecision, so be careful Gemini.
Too many options may be paralysing,
but don't let your energy stagnate;
you need to find a swift way out of
this one so you can keep going.

If squabbles and quarrels keep popping up all over the place, don't take them too much to heart. A little light firefighting, some gentle aftercare and before you know it peace will be restored once more.

Covering some ground is key right now Gemini – it's important to go far rather than just digging deep. Step away from intensity, to give your emotions a break, and uplift your energy with light and easy conversation. Keep flowing through.

If you feel that your energy is .
dragging, take early steps to reset and
replenish it. The last thing you need
right now is for things to get on top
of you; it's essential that you maintain
the inner strength and resources
you need to push through.

Embrace your own values, rather
than simply adopting those of others.
With your dual-minded nature it can
be a challenge sticking to one angle of
thought, and there's no reason you
should! However you do it, make sure
it's your own way.

Don't fall into the trap of people-pleasing this time Gemini – there's no way you can make everyone else agree with you, and, more to the point, why would you really want to? Conserve your energy for the part that really matters rather than chasing your tail about who thinks what and why.

With dual energy (and often dual viewpoints) at the heart of everything you do, tensions inevitably flare up now and again – both between you and others, and within yourself. Strive for balance and find the right approach (whether practical or emotional) for each situation.

Adapting to reach a compromise can be easier for you, Gemini, than it is for most; after all, who is more used to finding themselves in the middle of opposing viewpoints than you? If others are adopting a stubborn stance, find a more philosophical position for yourself and help them to see the best way forwards.

If you find yourself in a sticky spot, with something stopping you moving forwards, take a pause. Perhaps you are stopped here for a reason Gemini? Don't be too hasty about setting off again right away.

Pay attention to what your
ego requires right now Gemini; if
you find you are in need of a little
boost, seek out some supportive
company and share some of
your recent successes.

Small triumphs are the best sort; they are in ready supply for you Gemini, and trickle in steadily, bolstering your confidence along the way. Be sure you acknowledge them and the important role they play in keeping everything ticking over smoothly.

If everything feels like it might overwhelm you, take some time out and talk your issues through with friends and supporters. Ruled by such duality, it can sometimes seem that making any single decision is simply too hard on your own.

When faced with difficult personalities, look for the benefit they bring to your life. Coming up empty? Tolerate them for the minimum time possible, then make a break for it. You don't need to put yourself through that.

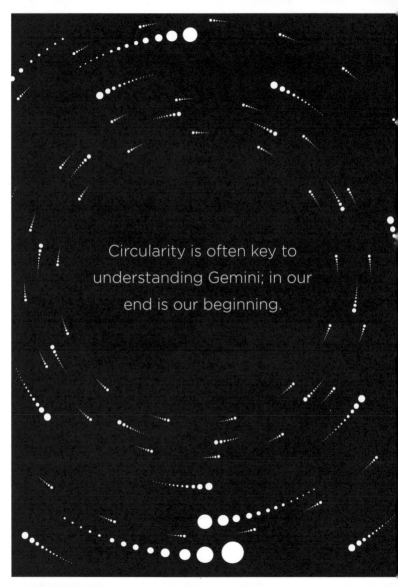

Circularity is often key to understanding Gemini; in our end is our beginning.

Communication is key to working all this through Gemini, and with several different sources. Bear in mind though that there may not be just one definite outcome. Most likely, you will need to patchwork together a new solution from different pieces of the answer; your response will be all the more robust for it.

Be especially mindful of the
words coming out of your mouth at
the moment Gemini. While it might
feel good to be engaged and
communicating, remember that
listeners might be taking your words
at face value and expecting some
impossibly impressive outcomes
as a result.

Feeling constrained, restricted
or controlled by a situation that is not
of your own making or choosing might
be adding to your frustration levels
Gemini. Find a way to vent that won't
cause any damage and prepare to
learn a few lessons about managing
your own temper.

Concentrate your efforts on sorting your affairs Gemini. It's important to be sure you are on top of all the different aspects of your life before you move on with this next phase.

Share what you have learnt with others who might be now where you were then. Be generous. Spreading this new world view will have immensely positive and far-reaching effects. Don't give up if they seem a little unwilling to hear you at first.

Keep talking with those you hope to influence Gemini, it is the only way that things will change. Support, suggestions, understanding and the weight of your own opinions will work their magic eventually.

It might be time to try something new, Gemini... how about a blend of some of your favourite things: socializing and travel? Sprinkle some education into the mix and you may very well have just what the doctor ordered.

This situation presents a great opportunity to re-evaluate and realign your goals Gemini; if it seems you have been overreaching, perhaps now is the time to pull back and work towards some more achievable interim targets.

Feeling stretched and frustrated are clear indicators that you are trying to do too much with too little. Whatever way this is playing out – whether at home, at work, in your personal goals, in relationships, or to do with finances – it is time to rein it in.

Being the life and soul of the party
is one thing Gemini, but there is more
to life than that (yes, really). Don't
forget to feather your own nest at the
same time as you are making sure
everyone else has room to spread
their wings, otherwise you will be
the one left behind.

Negative motivators are never
as powerful or successful as the
positives for you Gemini; you would
always prefer to welcome in the good
rather than pulling up the drawbridge
against the bad. Look carefully at the
current situation to see whether you
could be motivated differently.

More often than not you are
ready for action and primed to face
any opportunity that comes your way
Gemini. Be mindful that others might
not feel the same way and may not
appreciate being spoken for; you
shouldn't accept a new challenge or
additional work on anyone's behalf
except your own.

You love attention Gemini, and centre stage is your home from home. Be careful you don't allow a wave of sudden admiration to twist your focus away from the task at hand; don't be distracted by flattery.

Look for lasting value in all
the ventures you are pursuing
right now Gemini, whether in work,
relationships, investments or even love.
Quick-burning sparkle is fun for a few
moments, but then you're right back
where you started. Time to put some
building blocks in place.

The opportunity to make some great connections is on the cards Gemini... let's be honest, with your charm and warmth, when is it not? But if your intuition alerts you to something particularly special, be sure to pay close attention. Act accordingly.

Intense feelings can drain both your energy and your confidence Gemini; this isn't the way you like to feel and it's certainly not how you want others to see you. Take time to retreat and process your emotions and responses in your own space and time; then come back out into the main action when you are feeling more balanced.

It might be that you are facing bigger emotional waves than you can tackle alone Gemini. Call in some support from family or trusted friends, and when it comes to telling them the circumstances and the way you are feeling, don't skimp on the details. With a little help, plain sailing will be resumed before you know it.

Face forwards Gemini; as the ultimate buddy, you twins know a thing or two about the power of positivity. Keep yourself, and those around you, on track by focusing on the stages to come rather than squelching about in the muddy patches of the past. Onwards, Gemini. All will be well. The future is bright.

Vision, mission and accomplishment
– the magic equation for knocking
everyone out of their holding patterns
and doing what you do best Gemini:
making it happen! Time to start some
action and get this moving.

Working with others to make
something beautiful happen really
does it for you Gemini... as long as
they remember it was your idea, of
course. You're committed to your
vision and you want the world to know
it, so be bold and claim it as your
own the whole way through.

You might feel that others are not seeing you as you truly are Gemini, or perhaps that they are misinterpreting the duality of your nature as something more manipulative than it really is. Either way, if you think the image they have of you is clouded, take the first opportunity to wipe the lens and clear things up.

Refresh your understanding as
well as your perspective by taking in a
different view today Gemini.

If someone close to you is upset
or dissatisfied, and you are implicated
in some way, allow them the time they
need before attempting to explain
your position. Misunderstandings
are more easily corrected when
heads have cooled.

When tensions are running high it's a good idea to keep your head down and take cover... if only it were that easy for a Gemini. Stick to your own lane at least and try not to get caught up in other people's dramas, fascinating and enticing though they may look from outside.

Time to line up your goals and your outgoings Gemini – both literal and metaphorical – and take a look at whether there are any non-essentials you could cut back on at the moment.

If conflicts arise and your emotional reactions are strong, deal first with your physical response and adrenaline (by engaging in some good sweat-inducing exercise) and then settle down to deal with the issues from a calmer, more balanced and compassionate place. Use love rather than anger Gemini.

The universe has some big plans in store for you Gemini. Fasten your seatbelt; it's going to be a wild ride.

You may feel something is missing between where you are now and where you want to be Gemini. A contact from your past might be able to help you bridge that gap.

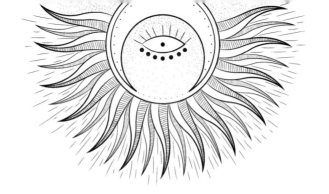

Stay alert to the unfamiliar
Gemini, new directions may come
courtesy of an unexpected source.
Keep your eyes open.

Memories of things we left
undone or unexplored can haunt us
just as surely as mistakes made.
Be brave and take a chance Gemini.

Returning to a familiar setting or arrangement may be key Gemini. Keep an open mind regarding how and where things should take place.

Missing links can take many forms Gemini; when you are seeking to finish a chain or secure a connection, bear in mind the experiences that others have shared and the support they can offer.

Despite your love of company, it is crucial that you switch back to basics sometimes Gemini, and spend some solo time reconnecting with yourself.

The way others judge you might sting a little Gemini, if it is not in your favour. But remember that those who feel compelled to disseminate their opinions in this way are ultimately only tarnishing their own reputations. It's just a shame it often doesn't feel that way at the time.

Take some time to reaffirm your commitment to a goal Gemini; it will help you maintain momentum.

Others may be noticing the results of a change you started quietly working towards a while ago. Smile and accept their compliments, but don't become complacent. There is still a way to go.

A lack of confidence isn't something you tend to struggle with Gemini, but a boost now may serve as an extra push towards the finish line. There is no shortage of support.

Your physical and mental health are inextricably intertwined Gemini, and you have been really drawing on your reserves recently. Now might be the time to think about refilling the tank.

Objective feedback will be tremendously valuable right now Gemini. Just be sure to set your ego aside and prepare a space for resulting advice to land, while you ready yourself to deal with it.

Time to prove you have what it takes. Never mind what others think, this one you need to achieve for yourself Gemini.

Versatile and fun-loving, you
are super-popular and never short
of companions. The changeability
inherent in your dual Gemini nature
can be confusing for others though, so
if there is a particular person you
would like to be closer to you should
share the things that anchor you.

Open-minded and never boring,
you need a stimulating environment
if you are to thrive Gemini.
Don't settle for less.

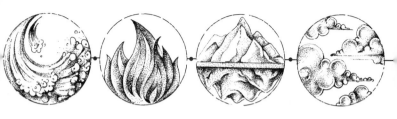

An air sign, and ruled by Mercury,
the urge to connect flows through
everything you do Gemini. Calming
your restless spirit might prove
challenging, but know that you are
complete as you are. That thirst for
'more' can be quenched.

Communication is essential to
a Gemini, and your quest for new
friends and connections will lead you
into many fascinating conversations. If
others have confided in you, think
twice before using their secrets
as a springboard for your
next anecdote.

Turmoil in your day-to-day
environment might be upsetting but
it is necessary at the moment Gemini.
Ride it out.

Mercury, the messenger of the zodiac, is responsible for your love of news and updates – there's nothing quite as satisfying as being on top of everything that's going on. Remind yourself now and then, though, that the more you talk the more others will hear. Get your facts straight first.

Things you think of as minor
issues might seem like big problems
to others. Allow for the fact that there
will be different takes on this before
you wade in Gemini.

Choose a strategic approach
over a messy confrontation Gemini;
keep things tidy and they will be much
easier to file neatly away once
this is all over.

Your light is shining as brightly as ever
Gemini – don't be tempted to dim it
just for the sake of fitting in.

Unsurprisingly Gemini, it's likely
to be you who has all the answers.
Others might be confused or even
upset by the current situation, but
pleasingly you will find that you are in
a position to make everything all right.

What looks like an
insurmountable barrier to
others may seem nothing more
than an easy step-over to you Gemini.
Your reassurances will go a long way
towards calming this situation.

You are not easily deceived Gemini, and your dual-facing nature means that not much escapes you. If someone is disingenuously attempting to manipulate the situation, nip it in the bud.

Difficulties that appear
at the beginning might magically
melt away as things progress and
warm up. Don't allow a tricky-looking
start to put you off.

Insights will flow, just as soon
as you let go of that tight grip on
what you think you want. Once you
have come to terms with how things
really are, everything will seem
looser and more possible.

Your insatiable appetite for
exploring the world around you might
lead to feelings that time is too short
to do everything you want to. But
resist the urge to rush ahead.

Don't succumb to disillusion Gemini; the fact that something has been revealed to be not as you thought is simply an opportunity for consolidation rather than a crisis. Turn this to your advantage.

There's very little you like more than a good chat Gemini and, as one of the most skilled conversationalists in the zodiac, others love talking with you as well. Use your favourite talent to build up some strong new connections.

Putting time into building bonds
with like-minded people now will really
pay off in the future Gemini.

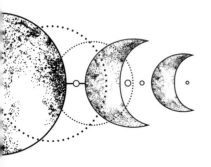

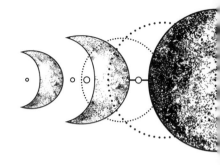

There's no better time for thinking big Gemini. Pouring creative energy into plans for the future will help you position yourself over the coming months.

With a super-full social life looking like it's about to become even busier, it seems you are on the cusp of big, exciting change Gemini. Conserve your strength and get ready to spread your wings.

Your boldness and bravery are
key to your brand. Don't be persuaded
to scale things back just to spare
someone else's ego. Let them enhance
their own game and step forwards to
meet you rather than requiring
you to step back.

New alliances will be key in
forging your path ahead Gemini.
Plenty of people will be able to help
you and, knowing you, you will make
some fantastic new friends along the
way as well. Stay open, honest
and listen carefully.

Broad and far-reaching as
your comfort zone is already, there is
always a little bit further you can push
to expand your horizons. Extra
planning will really pay off.

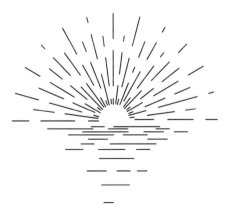

Important decisions will need
to be made soon Gemini; for now,
though, you should keep your eyes
and ears open, so you are fully
prepared when the time comes.

Focus on home and family can
go one of two ways for you Gemini
– pulling inwards in contentment or
pushing outwards to make a change.
Be honest about what you really need.

Finding the right path forwards will be easiest if you remain open to all the options, but then stick to your choice once it is made. There will inevitably be plenty of distractions along the way, and no doubt some of them will look pretty tempting.

The power of persuasion is strong
with you Gemini, and your wit and
warmth guarantee that others are
keen to come along for the ride.
Use your advantage wisely.

Surprises are in store for you Gemini; although you may have an inkling, keep it to yourself.

Be sure to retain an open
mind and embrace new ideas and
possibilities wholeheartedly. Chance
is on your side, but you must give
her a helping hand.

A regular reminder to regroup and reassess your own priorities is an essential calendar item Gemini. Build in the time to refresh and update your goals list every so often.

Love is the answer Gemini.
Happiness will come and go, and
bliss is necessarily fleeting. But love
will see you through. Nurture it.

First published in Great Britain in 2021 by
Greenfinch
An imprint of Quercus Editions Ltd
Carmelite House
50 Victoria Embankment
London EC4Y 0DZ

An Hachette UK company

A CIP catalogue record for this book is available
from the British Library

HB ISBN 978-1-52941-231-4

10 9 8 7 6 5 4 3 2 1

Designed by Ginny Zeal
Cover design by Andrew Smith
Text by Susan Kelly
All images from Shutterstock.com

Printed and bound in China.

Papers used by Greenfinch are from well-managed forests
and other responsible sources.